I CRY NO MORE

Beatrice Cunningham-Davis

1-31-2000

By Beatrice Cunningham-Davis

Published and Distributed by:
Milligan Books
an imprint of Professional Business Consultants
1425 W. Manchester, Suite C
Los Angeles, California 90047
(323) 750-3592

Cover Design By
Anthony Clark Moore & Associates

Formatting By
AbarCo Business Services

First Printing, January 2000
10 9 8 7 6 5 4 3 2 1

ISBN 1-881524-64-7

DEDICATION

This book is dedicated to all families who have experience the murder of their child or loved one.

Table Of Contents

Acknowledgment

To God be the glory, without Him I can do nothing but through Him all things are possible. It is the word of God that sustains us as we move through our lives on this planet.

I am grateful to the late Malva Johnson, who passed away in 1996. It was her words of encouragement that gave me the extra push to go forward as a writer.

To my mother, Gradie Burks, who supplied a wealth of information and had no idea that information was being compiled into a book. Thank you, mother.

To my daughter, Anthea Harrell, for her powerful contribution. Also, thank you for my grandbabies, Darien and Jessica Harell.

To my husband, Ray Davis, thank you for being yourself and allowing me to be free to be me.

To Dr. Rosie Milligan, thank you for encouraging me to tell my story.

To John Milligan, Sr., thanks for the tremendous effort put forth towards the completion of my book. I will be forever grateful.

To all who have experienced similar traumatic events in their lives. It is my hope that by sharing my pain and sorrow with you, you will be enabled to move forward on your journey through Life, in peace, through Jesus Christ.

About The Author

A native of Tulsa Oklahoma, I received a Bachelor's Degree in Elementary Education from Langston University. I now reside in Inglewood, California.

In 1985, my 15-year-old son was killed in a drive-by shooting. To this day, his murder remains unsolved; but God has given me the strength to go on with my life. Out of the pain and loss bloomed something beautiful, something to help me honor my son's life. I opened a Residential Facility for teenage boys. I was also inspired to write about the pain, the anger, the hurt, the unanswered questions, and above all, the will to live on after the death of my son.

I wrote this book knowing it may not soothe or ease your pain; I wrote with the hope that it would encourage you, the reader, to live on. I also wanted you to know that you are not alone; this kind of tragedy happens on a regular basis, but you can overcome it and LIVE ON!

Chapter 1

I followed the ambulance to the hospital. I don't know how I did it because my tears were blinding me. All I know is that when the ambulance ran red lights and stop signs, so did I. It was as if I was hitched to the back of the speeding vehicle and being towed. That's how close I was to it.

With the siren going, their lights flashing, and the tears streaming down my face, I felt as though my whole world was being shattered and thrown off course before my very eyes. And there was nothing I could do about it. I began to pray. I prayed like I had never prayed before, pleading to God. Please don't let my baby die. He is only 15 years old and hasn't had a chance to live his life. Please, God, give him another chance. Please don't take my baby. Not now. I said those words over and over until I couldn't say them any more.

As I continued to speed behind the ambulance, fear had consumed my entire body. I felt sick to my stomach. It was as if all hell had broken loose and I was being taken on a horror ride and had no control over the outcome. And the worst part was I didn't know whether my son was dead or alive. The only thing I knew was that my baby had been shot. Shot how? By whom? What gun? I have never owned a gun in my life. Those questions raced through my mind but no matter where my thoughts took me in my quest for understanding, I felt like I was staring into a black hole. That blackness lasted only a matter of seconds, and when the light showed through, it was like I was looking through the lens of a camera. What I saw was so horrifying that I cried out, "My Lord and My God." In the twinkling of an eye, I saw everything that had occurred leading up to that horrible day. I began to feel even sicker. All I could say was, "Oh, my God. How could I have let these things go by me? What could have been going through my mind? It was as if another force had control of me. Because there is no way that I should not have taken notice. Oh, my God, is this what you were trying to prepare me for, this day?"

You know my life was going in a direction that seemed right to me, and in the next moment it was as if all hell had broken loose, and I hadn't seen it coming. I read about and heard about these tragedies happening to other people, but I thought I was so far removed. When I heard about tragic things happening to other people, I would say, "That is so sad," or "I feel sorry for the family," and then I would go right on with my life. But, I never would have thought in my wildest dreams that it would or could happen to me. Now I truly understand the statement, "There, but for the grace of God, go I." Now I know that tragedy can happen to any of us. I have more than sympathy for those who have lost their children or loved ones. I can relate. When I hear a person who has not lost a child say, "I know how you feel," I know that is not true. I know they are trying to relate and sympathize with the situation the best they know how, but they don't know. I know for sure that I would never again tell a person I know how he or she feels unless I had experienced a similar or the same situation. I can imagine that we have all had a loss in our lives, but until I experienced the loss of my son, I could never imagine the pain and agony. It's just unimaginable. Honey baby, there ain't no words on God's green earth to truly express that pain. It is something that I wouldn't wish on my worst enemy.

Chapter 2

It has been very hard after all these years, trying to move on with my life, with the memories and guilt still in the forefront of my mind. It has been very hard trying to put it behind me. I know these scars will be with me to my grave. But no matter what I try to do, there is really nothing that I can do to change anything. I am gradually beginning to understand that what happened, happened.

So I am ready to go on with my life. Actually, I believe I have done that to a certain extent. But the memories of my son are always with me, especially when I see children of the same age as my son was at his death.

I know that death is not something that happens today, and tomorrow we can cast it out of our minds and go on with our lives as if nothing has happened. No, it takes time, and however long it takes will basically depend on the individual.

17

As I begin to heal, I know there are certain things I have to face so that I can allow myself to go on. I have been unwilling to look back at all that has happened. And I know that I will never have closure until I do this. It is time for me to release my son from my mind, but he will always be a part of my heart. He has already found his peace, now I must find mine.

Until now, I have never wanted to actually face this head on to try to get some type of understanding as to what it all meant. I was so bitter that it happened, that I didn't want to talk about it. Everytime my daughter would try to spark a conversation, relating to the situation, or reminisce about herself and her brother, I would immediately change the subject or not respond at all. I couldn't go back there, it was still too painful for me. I believe that I needed to recover in my own way and time.

I have searched high and low, trying to find a way to alleviate this never-ending pain and to fill the deep void in my heart. In my search, I became someone that I did not like, and you can imagine what the people in my life were dealing with. I was so filled with despair that it showed in everything that I attempted to do, and there were times I did not want to do a whole heck of a lot. I worked because I needed the money. For years, I had loved my job, but the joy was no longer there.

No matter what I did, I hurt. I was even hurting after I thought I didn't hurt any more. It showed on my face. There wasn't a day that went by without some kind of constant reminder of him. I remember many times being out and being approached by strangers who would walk up to me and say, "Smile, it can't be that bad." I was always surprised when that happened, because I had no idea that I looked any different. I would ask myself, what are they talking about? There's nothing wrong with me. And besides, who walks around with a smile plastered to their face all the time? Many times I became irritated by the remarks. I just wanted to be left alone. Deep down, I knew that I was only fooling myself.

But it wasn't until I kept going through the same ordeal, that I began to understand this statement: we never see ourselves as other people see us. All the pain inside of me showed on my face.

In a strange way, this revelation helped me to become a people watcher. Focusing on others helped me to take my attention off my problem. And the sad thing I discovered was that so many people walk around with frowns on their faces. Some of the frowns looked like they were permanently implanted. I began to wonder if there were any happy people in the world.

I still remember one lady in particular. The look she had on her face made me want to cry. I could not imagine what she had been through or was going through, but her facial expression let me know that it was not good.

It was this woman, and all the many faces that I saw then and still see today, that made me check myself. It was then that I began to see in others what they saw in me.

We may not realize it, but we are all in this thing called life together. We need each other. Many times people are not willing to discuss their problems with you, and that is okay. But once you show some concern, your words may go a long way. Even though they may be in denial, they know what the truth is. We may not ever need to know.

Chapter 3

It was important for me to turn my grief into something positive. When I searched for the many things that I could do, I began to look at the young people in our community, especially the youth who had been taken from their homes and had nowhere to go. After a lot of planning, in 1990 I opened a residential home for boys. Though this couldn't take the place of my son, I felt good doing it. I knew I was making a positive difference in the lives of so many young men. But nothing I did really took my son's place. And to be truthful, there is nothing you can do that can replace a life that is gone. You can do things to make life bearable so that you can go on. I had to learn that. No matter how many children came through my placement, not one could take the place of my child. I continued to go on with my life. But I wasn't able to go on with my life the way I wanted to until I allowed Jesus into my life. Jesus made the difference. That's when I realized that I couldn't do a thing without Him. Scripture says, "I can do all things through Christ who strengthens me."

That's what has kept me, His strength. There were many times when I have wanted to lie down and give up. It took a lot of effort and energy not to do that. It took Jesus for me to press on. He helped turn my life around and has never left me. Jesus said that if we would take one step, He would take two. My, isn't that good news?

I am beginning to see things in a different light now. It is true what they say about time healing all wounds, but only if we allow it, and only if we do what we can to help ourselves. Again I recommend Jesus. In Matthew 11:28, Jesus says, "Come unto me all ye who labor and are heavy laden and I will give you rest." As I continued to read and rely on Him and His word, I began to know that the answers to every circumstance in life are contained in the Bible.

After 15 years, I can honestly say that I am ready to journey back to that part of my life. I know that it is not going to be easy, having to relive the past, especially when that past includes the death of a child. But it is important for me to do this, not only for myself, it is my hope that my story will be an inspiration for some and a blessing to others, especially to those who may have had similar experiences. I ask for God's continuing guidance as I move forth on my journey.

Chapter 4

Death began knocking at my door on May 2, 1985. I remember that day as if it were only yesterday. It was a typical day, nothing unusual. I got up at my normal time, got the kids ready for school, and went to work. Even at work, everything was normal. After work, I walked through the parking lot on my way to my car and greeted some of my co-workers as they began to leave. Then, I got into my car and drove off.

I remember thinking what a beautiful day it was. It was sunny; it was clear – I could see all the way to the mountains. The sound of birds chirping and the smell of spring flowers blooming seemed to fill the air. I thought what a wonderful day to just take a long drive and enjoy the beautiful scenery. I felt that great.

It wasn't one of those days when I was going home stressed from the problems at work. Not this day. I had a very positive attitude and was in a great mood.

Nothing was bugging me. When I say nothing, I mean absolutely nothing. I was tuned into my favorite radio station and just enjoying the oldies music. As I leaned back, I allowed my mind to be taken back to many pleasant memories, remembering what I was doing when I first heard that song and even remembering what dances were popular then. I smiled as I sang along, remembering all the words. (Even after all these years!)

As the memories in my mind continued to build, the songs reminded me of people I had grown up with. I began to wonder about them. What were they all doing now? I hope life had treated them well. I wondered if any of them ever wondered about me?

Even the traffic was light that day, which was unusual for the normally packed freeway. Usually cars were swerving in and out of lanes. I thought, okay this must be my lucky day. I will probably get home a few minutes early. Then I began to make plans for the evening. I thought, as soon as I get home, I'm going to kick off my shoes, kick back and chill for a spell before going into phase two. You know, pre-paring dinner, helping with the homework and whatever else that may need my attention.

I realized my exit was coming up soon, and before I could set my thoughts into orbit again, something strange began to happen to me. Out of the clear blue sky, this very depressing feeling came over me. It came for no apparent reason. I couldn't imagine what it could be. I thought that maybe I was catching a virus or something. But that didn't make sense. I didn't feel ill. This feeling was so strange and so sudden; it was as if something had invaded my body. I had no control over this feeling. It deeply saddened me. It was so sad, that my spirit dropped in an instant. It went down real low. The best way to describe this is by saying that it was the type of feeling you get when you have been told that your children, or mother or father, is dead or dying. It was a feeling of death. It was as if someone had communicated these words to me in a whisper, "Someone is going to die." For a moment, I began to think that someone was in the car. But of course, that was ridiculous and I knew it. The message came with great power and authority, as if my attention was demanded, whether or not I wanted to listen, But hear this! It was as if I had no choice in the matter but to listen.

The episode did not last long, perhaps a few seconds at the most. It went as quickly as it came. That was one of the most frightening things I have ever experienced. At that point, I did the only thing I knew to do. I just kept on driving. Can you imagine driving along and suddenly a message is communicated to you about death? I could not have imagined it either until it happened to me.

I tried to make some kind of sense of this, but I had nothing to work with since the message did not come through normal channels – like from one human being to another. I really did not want to accept it. But there was something inside of me that led me to believe that this was real. That's what had me so frightened.

In my mind, I had already begun to respond to the message. For some reason, the response was spontaneous, and not of my own will. It was as if I was dealing with two forces. One force knew the truth and the other force was operating out of fear and caused me to fight back.

I began to think and react as if I had been told by the doctor that I had a short time to live. The first thought that came to mind was that I needed to get my business in order. I automatically assumed the message was about me. I made that assumption out of fear. I was so frightened when I heard those words; someone was going to die. I immediately put up a mental block. I closed my ears and my mind. I had heard enough. I did not want to hear anymore. I could not bear the thought that it might be about my children, mother or any family members. Just the mere thought saddened me so. That's the reason I automatically assumed the message was about me. That was the way I wanted it to be. That was the only way I could handle it. I was too afraid to wonder beyond myself. The fear in me was so strong, that this was my way of taking control. So, my thoughts were, "Here I am, Lord, take me." I wanted my family to be left alone.

Then, I began to wonder how was my death going to occur? So far, I had no known illnesses. Would I suffer a violent death at the hands of another? Would I be involved in an accident?

Then, I began to think about my children. How could I die and leave them behind? Who would care for them? Their father and I were divorced and he was having a difficult time taking care of himself. It was those thoughts and others that continued to run through my mind.

But the one thing that continued to stand out in my mind was the fact that I needed to get my business in order. I know how important that is. It had been in the back of my mind for a long time. I just never labeled it a priority. I had heard many horror stories from others regarding loved ones who died before taking care of business. So, I just took this message as a reminder.

By the time I reached home, I was drained emotionally. I felt like I had been in a mental battle. For about five minutes, I just sat in my car trying to figure out what the heck had happened? What was that all about? I cannot believe what I just went through. Am I losing my mind or what? I was so exhausted that I felt like I had walked home.

I certainly didn't plan to share this experience with anyone, especially my friends, and then have to listen to them talk out the side of their mouths. I knew they would say things like, "Girl, you must have been tripping really hard that day." Or, "A voice told you do what? Girl, that voice you're talking about didn't mention my name, did it?" They would make a mockery out of what happened to me. I have learned you are better off keeping certain things to yourself. Especially since I was having a difficult time believing it myself.

So, I decided that it was just a thought, which had no validity. Thoughts come and thoughts go. When thoughts entered my mind and there was no place for them in my life, I dismissed them. And that's exactly with I did with this thought.

The sad part about all of this is that the time and date had already been set. So no matter what I did or failed to do, it was not going to make a difference. But I did not know this.

Finally I got out of my car and went into the house as if nothing had ever happened.

As the days rolled on, I never thought about what happened again. But I never relinquished the thought that I needed to get my business in order. But it seemed like every time I decided to address the issue, something else would pop up and fill that slot. I just could not understand my procrastination; that was not my nature. So the longer I prolonged it, the further it got from my mind. Finally, I forgot about it.

Chapter 5

A bout a week after the occurrence on the freeway, my children and I were at home enjoying a good movie on the television, when the phone rang. We were so engrossed in the movie that no one wanted to move to answer it. I had to chuckle because, any other time, my children would have broken their necks to answer the phone. But nobody moved, so you know it had to have been a good movie. I decided that I was not going to answer it, especially with two teenagers in the house. Nine times out of ten, it wasn't for me anyway.

Finally, my daughter could no longer stand the suspense and answered the phone. I was surprised when she said, "It's for you, Mom." "Darn," I thought to myself. For a minute, I started to say take a message, but something said, "take the call." I did not ask who it was, expecting it to be someone that I knew. But when I said, "hello," to my surprise, it was an

unfamiliar male's voice. "Nope,"I said to myself, "not anybody I know."

He began introducing himself by saying
that a friend of mine referred him. I thought to
myself, "Yea, thanks a lot, friend, whomever
you are." But that wasn't the real kicker. He
said that he worked for a local cemetery selling
plots. I thought, "You definitely called the
wrong number."

He also said that his company was running a promotion and that the offer was good to
any one who took advantage of it by a certain
date. When I heard that, it took everything
inside of me not to become rude; during that
time in my life it was really hard for me to hold
myself back. So every now and then, I grunted
to let him know I was still on the line.

At the end of his sales pitch, he added that
I would realize even greater savings if I acted
quickly. Then he asked, "What time would be
better for you, mornings or evenings?" I thought
to myself, none of the above. I could realize
even greater savings by getting off this phone.
At that point, I was really vexed. First of all,
I was missing my movie, and second I don't
believe I gave him any indication that I was

interested. Third, I'm putting my money into something that is going to draw interest, not into the ground (so to speak) waiting for someone to die. Then I thought, "Why am I putting myself through this? Just tell him point blank, I am not interested. Have a good day and hang up the phone. And anyway no one is getting ready to die." He kept on jabbering away until finally my better side kicked in. I told him whatever he wanted to hear just to get off the phone. After all, he did sound like a nice guy and I had to realize that's how salespeople make their money. I too had been in sales for many years.

Against my better judgement, I did make an appointment for him to stop by, but I made him no promises. We said our good-byes and I was back to watching the movie.

I really felt bad after hanging up, because I knew that I wasn't going to buy anything, but I figured it didn't cost anything to listen.

After that, I never gave that conversation another thought. I get calls from people selling first one thing, then another, so why should I have thought any differently about this call?

Several days later, I ran into a friend at the post office, the one who was kind enough to refer me to the salesman. We laughed and joked about it. Then, we went on about our business.

About a week later, on Tuesday evening at approximately 5:30, the doorbell rang. I had just gotten home. I thought to myself, "Dang! People don't even give a person a chance to get home from work before they start ringing the door bell."

I thought it was some of the neighborhood kids looking for my son. Andre and his friends were always back and forth between each other's homes and I was sure it was just some of his friends.

Before I answered the door, I peeped out of the window knowing that I couldn't be too careful these days. To my surprise, it wasn't any of the kids or anyone that I knew. From where I was standing, I could see that it was a man. He appeared to be a salesman. He was carrying a briefcase and large folders. I started not to answer the door, but I felt he might have seen me peeping out the window. Before I opened the door, I asked, "May I help you?" He called my name. Who could that be? I asked myself.

When I opened the door, there stood a handsome, young Black man who was very well dressed. He appeared very confident as to his purpose for being at my door. He greeted me and handed me his card, as if I was supposed to know the rest. He immediately detected that I didn't have a clue as to his purpose for being there. He quickly triggered my memory, reminding me that we had an appointment for that day. Then, it came back. I apologized and invited him in, making excuses about why I had forgotten. We just laughed it off.

"Why am I putting myself through this?" I thought. I knew I was not going to buy anything. I could have avoided all of this just by telling him that day on the phone, "No thanks, I am not interested." I could have saved both of us a lot of time. But since he was there, I had to make the best of it.

I directed him to the dining table where he would have enough room to spread out his materials. We chatted for a bit while he got things situated. He commented on how spacious my house was. As we continued to talk, we found out that we had something in common. I knew his aunt. We had worked together a number of years before. I said, "Gosh, what a small world." He agreed.

He proceeded to show me pictures that represented the different burial plots that were available through the promotion. It was all very impressive, but in my mind we were talking about death. I began to feel an uneasiness come over me. Finally, I politely asked if he would quote me the different prices, and if I decided to purchase, I would pick the one with the lowest price. I thought, it's not like I'm buying a house or a car. What's the big deal?

His reply was, "In order to participate in the promotion and receive the discount, you have to listen to the entire presentation." He continued by saying, "I won't be much longer." I thought, well, I allowed him to come into my home, so I have to deal with it. I must admit he was very professional and knew his stuff.

Finally, he got to the money part, even though I was not interested. To my surprise, the plans were quite affordable. For some reason unknown to me, I decided to fill out the application. There was a part of me that said," Go ahead, it's good to be prepared, and by being prepared you can save yourself a lot of money in the long run." But there was the other side of me that said, "Don't do it. Take your chances and cross that bridge when you get to it." After completing the application, I let my fears rule. I got cold feet. I told him I needed a week to think about it. Of course, he was not too happy and he tried endlessly to persuade me to go through with it. He said we just never know. I felt bad for him, but it was not about him, it was about me. That was the chance I had to take. We agreed on a day to meet again the next week. He packed his things and left.

The thought of death frightened me so much, that I tried to deny everything about it. But what's interesting is that I did allow the young man to come and make his presentation. That meant something inside of me was responding to the message. Something inside of me was leading me to do what I was supposed to do, whether I acknowledged it or not. As I mentioned earlier, I felt like I was dealing with two forces. There was a part of me that knew I should take advantage of the plan. But there was a part of me that was putting up a big fight. And that part was fear. I don't know many people who have accepted death willingly: but fighting or ignoring things doesn't change the outcome of God's plan. I have often heard it said, "The things we fear the most are the things that will come upon us."

Chapter 6

Before I knew it, the salesman was back at my door. But this time I did not meet with him. I sent my nephew to tell him that I had decided not to go with his burial plan at this time. Disappointed as I knew he would be, he said, "Okay." Then he left. When I heard the door close, I felt relieved. I felt victorious.

I felt a sense of relief that I hadn't spend any money or created another bill. I had held on to my conviction. I didn't need that burial plot anyway. I had insurance on my children and myself, which was sufficient. Besides that, I did not know if I would continue to live in Los Angeles.

As you can see, out of fear I tried to justify my action. I made excuses for making the wrong decision. But I was fighting a battle that I was going to lose no matter what I did. The course had already been set that day on the freeway. I now believe that I was being spiritually guided. I believe the salesman did not come on his own. I believe he was sent to help me prepare for what was to come and he didn't know it.

Well, the warnings did not stop there. Two days later, I was in the kitchen washing dishes, when my nephew walked in with the news that he was getting ready to go back home. Home was in the Midwest. He came to live with us after graduating from high school.

My thought was perhaps he was homesick, but before I could think on anything else, he hit me with his prediction. He said, "Something is getting ready to happen to you." Though his words jolted me, I continued with what I was doing, not showing any type of emotion. He added that he was leaving the next week. I thought, next week is in two days. For a moment, I was speechless. I thought, who is he to come in here half-cocked trying to predict my future without details to substantiate it? I simply said, with an attitude, "Something has already happened to me."

I could tell by the look on his face that he was serious. He had always been known as the jokester, and I was hoping that he was just making a joke this time. But, he wasn't.

Even though he had already told me, I asked him again, "When did you say you were leaving?" I didn't want him to go, but I wasn't going to try and stop him. I thanked him for telling me and continued washing the dishes.

By the following weekend, my nephew was gone. Obviously, he saw what I failed to look at. He saw sorrow coming and he had every right to leave, if that was the way he had to handle it.

I continued with my life as I saw fit, trying to provide a good life for my kids and being totally unaware of the horror that lay ahead.

My son was becoming closer to his friends. They spent a lot of time raising pigeons. These were kids who lived in the neighborhood, and many of them were from single parent homes, just like Andre. They provided each other with support when they needed to talk and get things off their chests. I knew many of the parents. I thought they were all pretty swell kids. But I wish I had paid more attention. Especially to my son's words.

I made an appointment to take Andre to the orthodontist to have braces put on his teeth.

Once we got to the doctor's office, Andre began to act very strange. Even the doctor had a difficult time getting him to cooperate. Andre kept telling the doctor, "I don't know why my mom is wasting her money to have this done, because I won't be needing them." Can you imagine a child talking in that manner? I thought that he was worried about the way he would look with braces. I had the braces put on anyway. I just thought that mother knows best.

The school year was coming to a close and I wanted to make sure he had something to do to keep him busy over those few months. I took him on a job interview and was surprised when the man hired him on the spot. He was scheduled to begin working the following Monday. I think I was just as happy and excited as he was, maybe even more so. So, I reinforced what he already knew, that he would work and attend summer school. That would pretty much take up most of the day.

For as long as I live, I will never forget my son's response to me. He turned and looked at me with sadness in his eyes, then he said, "You think you have it all figured out, huh, Mom?" His words caught me off guard, to the point I was speechless. But I was so over-whelmed by his accomplishment that I did not respond. I felt that I had achieved what I had set out to do and that was to keep him busy during summer vacation. What he said just went over my head. I just tossed it in the pile with all the other warnings.

Yes, he was correct. I thought I had it all figured out. Now, I know that all those plans I had for him "ain't never gonna happen."

You know we make plans and expect things to go exactly the way we planned it and this is what we hope for. But if it is not in God's will for us, it will never happen. So, we should always say, if it is God's will, I will do thus and so. We, as parents, should listen to what our children have to say and respect their ideas and opinions. They have a lot to say and they need someone to listen. Don't wait until something happens and you are faced with these words...I tried to tell you, but you never would listen. You were always too busy, too tired, or on the phone. If you don't take the time to listen today, tomorrow may be too late. Because there is always someone out there willing to listen to your child, but it may not be in his or her best interest to listen to that particular someone.

Chapter 7

It was a Saturday, about 8 pm, and I was becoming a little uneasy because Andre had not come home. He had gone over to his friend's house and was supposed to be back before 8. It was so unlike him not to call. For the life of me, I could not find my telephone book to call and see what might have been the problem. My first instinct was to think the worst. My mind began making suggestions. Usually I don't carry on like this, I try to think positive. But really looking back, my spirit had uneasiness all that day. I couldn't just chill out like I would have liked to. I began to pray and ask God to help me with my child.

You know, we, as parents, think we know our kids so well that we think we can predict their do's and don'ts, their will's and wont's, and many times we do come close. We try to allow for a slight deviation and in someways that is good. But we must continue to let our kids know that we are on top of things like a navigator and scooping them all the way.

Thirty minutes later, I heard the door open and I sighed with relief. I yelled down-stairs, "Andre, is that you?" Of course, I knew it was him, who else would it be? But you never know. He answered in a weak voice, "Yes." I thanked the Lord.

When he saw my face, he knew I was not pleased, and I let him know that I wasn't. He was the type of kid that did not like to see me unhappy. He would do whatever he could to change that. After we had our talk, he assured me that it would not happen again. Then, he went to his room.

The next morning seemed to come very quickly. I had no idea at the time what life had in store for me. It was Sunday and Father's Day. I was saddened with thoughts of my children being without their father, even though I knew it was for the best, with all the arguments and tension.

I went into the kitchen to start breakfast, but to my surprise, Andre had gotten up before everyone, cleaned the house, and prepared breakfast for us. I was really surprised. I hugged and thanked him. I knew this was his way of repenting for last night. But not only that, that was just his way.

When we returned from church, I had to leave for about an hour. But before I left, Andre asked if he could go dirt bike riding with his friends. These were our friends and neighbors; they lived two houses down. I was shocked that he had the nerve to ask if he could go after what had happened the night before.

He said his friend's father was taking them. I hesitated for a moment, thinking about what had occurred the night before. My better judgment told me to say no, because he needed to take responsibility for his actions. But I let guilt come into play. I felt guilty and sorry for him because his father did not spend time with him. After confirming with my neighbor, I said yes, because I knew he would be in good hands.

My daughter was a homebody. I knew she would stay close to home. Before walking out the door, I hugged them and I told Andre to have fun. I said good-by and walked out the door.

Little did I know that would be the last time I would ever see my son alive. I had no idea that my good-bye meant good-bye, so long, I will never see you again, I will never see your smiling face.

As I was leaving my appointment, I noticed an obituary on the desk by the door. I picked it up and read it. It wasn't the words that astonished me; it was the picture of a beautiful young woman. I inquired as to who she was and I was told she had been a friend. She was 21 at her death. I became very sad. I felt so sorry that she had to die so very young and her parents, gosh, how sad. I placed the obituary back on the table, and then I proceeded to my car.

As I drove home, I could not take my mind off the obituary. Just the fact that she had to die so young stood out in my mind. I know death has no age limit, but still she was young. Then, I thought about her parents. I imagined how painful it was for them to have to bury a child. It was as if I could feel their pain. I knew death was inevitable. But, no matter how many times we are faced with the loss of a loved one, it hurts every time.

Before I knew it, I was home and pulling into the driveway. I honked my horn, as I always did to let my children know that I was home. After parking the car, I took a deep breath before getting out. I entered the house through the back door. Once I was inside the house, I called out, but no one answered.

I assumed that Andre had already gone and Anthea was upstairs sleeping. I placed my purse and keys on the kitchen table and proceeded to go upstairs to check on her. From the side of my eye, I caught a glimpse of a white paper lying on the back of the sofa. I picked it up and immediately recognized my daughter's handwriting. Before reading the message, I assumed she was letting me know where she was. But that was not the case at all. As I read the message, I panicked; my heart began beating faster. I could not believe what I was reading. It made no sense to me.

The note stated that my son had been shot over on Mullen Street, which was three blocks from where we lived. I immediately grabbed my purse, keys, and ran frantically out the door and into my car. I was so nervous, I could hardly put the key into the ignition. Tears were streaming down my face.

I said, "Okay, I need to remain calm." But, how do you do that after receiving that type of message? I kept telling myself that it wasn't bad, probably a shot in the leg or arm, or something minor. But I still could not believe she said he was shot. It just wasn't registering.

Even though I was only three blocks away, it seemed like I could not get there fast enough.

When I turned the corner of Mullen, I could see the ambulance was there. I pulled up behind them and tried to park, but the paramedics motioned for me to move because they were getting ready to leave. I yelled out that I was his mother and asked where they were taking him. They gave me the name of the hospital. I knew the location. I backed my car away and waited for them to pull out.

I followed the ambulance to the hospital. I don't know how I did it because my tears were blinding me. All I know is that when the ambulance ran red lights and stop signs, so did I. It was as if I was hitched to the back of the speeding vehicle and being towed. That's how close I was to it.

With the siren going, their lights flashing, and the tears streaming down my face, I felt as though my whole world was being shattered and thrown off course before my very eyes. And there was nothing I could do about it. I began to pray. I prayed like I had never prayed before, pleading to God. Please don't let my baby die. He is only 15 years old and hasn't had a chance to live his life. Please, God, give him another chance. Please don't take my baby. Not now. I said those words over and over until I couldn't say them any more.

As I continued to speed behind the ambulance, fear consumed my entire body. I felt sick to my stomach. It was as if all hell had broken loose and I was being taken on a horror ride and had no control over the outcome. And the worst part was I didn't know whether my son was dead or alive. The only thing I knew was that he had been shot. Shot how? By whom? What gun? I have never owned a gun in my life. Those questions raced through my mind but no matter where my thoughts took me in my quest for understanding, I felt like I was staring into a black hole. That blackness lasted only a matter of seconds, and when the light showed through, it was like looking through the lens of a camera. What I saw was so horrifying that I cried out, "My Lord and My God." In the twinkling of an eye, I saw everything that had occurred leading up to that horrible day. I began to feel even sicker. I just could not believe all this was happening to me.

The hospital was only a few miles away, but it seemed like it took forever to get there. I pulled in the emergency parking lot, then parked my car in the first available spot. I was so nervous that when I got out of the car, I closed the door and left the engine running. Luckily, I did not lock the door.

After turning the ignition off, I ran frantically into the hospital in hopes of catching up with the paramedics who had already wheeled Andre from the ambulance and through the large swinging doors leading to the emergency room. I didn't even get a chance to see him.

I spoke with the receptionist and she directed me to the waiting area. She said someone would be with me shortly. I thanked her and sat down, trying to sort all of this out in my mind. What could have possibly happened? But, I was unable to concentrate. My mind was on my son. But at that moment, what had happened was not nearly as important to me as knowing how my child was doing.

I began pacing the floor. Minutes seemed like hours. Finally, a nice-looking lady came into the room and introduced herself as the hospital Social Worker. She was very pleasant and I could hear the sympathy in her voice.

She asked me if I was okay and if I needed to use the telephone. I told her I was doing as well as could be expected under the circumstances and that I was very concerned about my son. She apologized, but said that she did not have any information regarding his condition. But she assured me that the doctor would come to speak with me soon. In times like these, soon seemed like an eternity.

She had forms that needed to be filled out regarding insurance information. I supplied her with the information she needed. Then, I signed it. She finally asked me how did my son get shot? I hesitated for a second, and then I told her that I did not know. Her response was that she was sorry. As she prepared to leave the room, she reassured me again that it was okay for me to use the telephone. And, she reminded me that the doctor would be in shortly. I could tell that she felt sorry for me. Then she left.

Finally, I decided to take her up on her offer. I called my family in Oklahoma to let them know what had occurred. To let them know as much as I knew. Before hanging up, I promised to keep them informed. In times like these, it's good to have someone to talk with.

No sooner had I hung up the phone then the doctor walked in. He introduced himself and asked if I was the parent of the fifteen-year-old that had been brought in with the gunshot wound. I said, "Yes, I am Andre's mother." Immediately, I detected something in his voice. His entire demeanor scared me. After I answered his question, I did not say any more.

I immediately detected that something was wrong when he gave me no eye contact. And the way he rambled on and on about the extent of the injury instead of getting to the point. He sounded like he was trying to justify something and at the same time he was being apologetic. I felt that I was at the edge and about to fall off. I guess he was trying to find the right words, but there were no right words to break the news to me. But these were my thoughts afterward. Regardless, I never gave up hope. He explained that the bullet had gone in through his chest and ricocheted through his stomach.

It was at that point, that I saw the sorrow in his eyes when he looked straight into mine. But it was the words that he spoke that rocked my world. "I'm sorry, but your son did not make it. He's dead." No sooner did those words pass from his lips, then the pain struck me with such centrifugal force, that I felt as if an arrow had pierced right through my heart. The pain magnified with each breath I took. I moaned and I groaned. That pain was more than one person should have to bear. I felt like my heart had been ripped from my body and I was wearing it on the outside. I yelled out to God, "You took my baby away from me!" Silence had overcome the room. When I gained control, I looked at the doctor and said, " Sir, there has to be a mistake. He was only fifteen years old. He hasn't had a chance to live his life. I had so many plans for him. Now you are telling me they are never going to happen?" I repeated these words again "My son is too young to die and he would not leave me just like that." The doctor looked at me sadly then said that he was sorry. He had done all he could do to save my son. I know that it was very hard for him having to deliver that message. But it wasn't as hard as it had been for me to receive it.

I rose to my feet. I had no more business there. There was no reason for me to hang around any longer. As I prepared to leave the waiting room, the doctor asked if I wanted to see my son. I hesitated for a second, then I shook my head. I was hurt, I was angry. I was angry with the doctor for letting him die. At that point, I did not comprehend what he was saying to me. In my mind, I was dealing with the reality of it. I wanted to say to the doctor, "You just said my son was dead. What is there to see?"

My son was full of life, able to breathe, smile and talk. How can I look at him in the absence of all of that? I was helpless. I felt like I was bound, tied-up and gagged. I gave my son life, but that was no longer in my power. I was standing in the middle of helplessness. I was angry with the doctor and his inability to save my son's life.

Deep down, I wanted to see him. This was my child, my baby boy. I really wanted to see Andre, but I did not have the strength to see him like that. Not at that moment. I just couldn't handle it, seeing him lying there unable to speak, not breathing, dead. I consider myself a strong person, but certain things take more than strength. As I headed for the door, the doctor asked if there was anyone he could call for me. I said, "No, but thanks anyway."

Then, I was out the door. That was the hardest thing I ever had to endure in my life. Having to walk out of that hospital knowing that my child, my own flesh and blood, was stretched on the table dead because someone had shot him. I just didn't understand. Part of my life was gone forever, nothing would ever be the same. I asked myself what had I done to make this race so hard to run. It was then that I began to realize that the thing I feared the most had come upon me. And that was the death of my child. This is what I had refused to look at. My child's death.

When I walked out of the hospital, I was dazed and confused. My head was pounding. This had been such a horrible day. I felt like I had been watching a horror movie on television, but this time, the camera was on me.

As I headed to my car, I felt so alone. Suddenly, I heard someone calling my name. I couldn't imagine who would be calling me. When I looked around, I saw my dear friend, Joe, and her husband. And to my surprise, my daughter was in the car with them.

I was so relieved to know that she was okay. Despite all that had happened, I had never been so happy to see them. I guess by the look on my face they could detect that the news was not good, but I don't think they expected to hear what I was about to tell them. I hesitated for a minute, then I said, "Andre is dead. He did not make it." Those were the hardest words for me to utter. Hearing them still didn't make it real. My daughter cried and cried. I felt so sorry for her. Besides losing her brother, she had lost her best friend. I wondered what could I do or say to her to make her feel better. But I drew a blank. Her pain was my pain and all we had was each other.

My friend offered to drive my daughter and me home in my car. I thanked her because I knew I wasn't in the mood for driving. As we rode along, she did her best to console us with her words of wisdom. I will be forever grateful, but I couldn't tune in. In times like these there are no words to ease the pain. But it's good to know that people care. I have often heard it stated that, "Time heals all wounds." But no one could have convinced me of that then.

My mind flashed back to the obituary and I remembered my sadness. I knew then that the grief I was feeling for this family was the sadness for my own grief. I believe that Andre was shot at the same time I picked up the obituary and read it.

When we arrived at my house, I looked at it and realized Andre would never again stand on the balcony, looking over, talking to his friends as he had done so many times. Just to see him standing there always brought joy to my heart, knowing that he was home and safe. That was all gone now. Nothing looked the same. Not the house, the street...everything seemed so dismal. But I knew it was just me. I asked myself, "What do I do now?" And I answered my own question – nothing. I didn't seem to know what to do with myself. In my mind, I wanted to go and look for him, but look where? Finally, I took a deep and agonizing breath. It even hurt to breathe.

My friend Joe parked the car and I took my time getting out. I saw no reason to rush. I stepped out of the car and no sooner did I put both feet on the ground then a strange feeling came over me. It was as if a weight had been lifted from my shoulders.

I didn't make a big deal out of it. I briefly mentioned it to Joe. I felt whatever the meaning was, it didn't matter to me. It was all over any way. My feelings were, I hadn't listened to any of the messages before his death when perhaps I could have made a difference. Now, it was too late.

We went into the house. I went upstairs because I wanted to be alone. About 30 minutes later, Andre's father was at the door. As I was coming down the stairs, I overheard him tell Anthea that after he got the news of Andre's death, a strange feeling came over him. He described it as something lifting from his shoulders. It was identical to what I had experienced. I never commented to my ex-husband about what I had felt, because it no longer mattered.

God has His way of doing things, and none of us have the answers as to why. But I knew that my baby was gone. Reason and explanations will never change that or ease the pain. Our lives are like vapors – one second we're here, and then the next second we're gone. But I never thought my child would precede me in death.

I went back upstairs into Andre's room. I looked at his pictures. The only thing I had left was an image of what was. He was a very cute baby. His hair was coal black. He was a long baby. I knew he was going to be tall like his father. I remember when he was eight months old. He would climb out of the baby bed. I thought that was the strangest thing. Gosh, I had such pleasant memories of his life and at the same time I was faced with his death. I will never see that smile again or his beautiful brown eyes staring at me. I will never be able to talk to him or hear him call me Mom or hold him in my arms to let him know that everything is going to be all right. It's all gone. As I sat on his bed and looked around the room, I realized that those clothes in the closet no longer had an owner. They belonged to no one. No one would live in this room any longer. The previous occupant, who had found his way back home, had abandoned it. Knowing Andre, I was sure that if it was at all possible, he was looking down and saying, "Don't cry, Mom. I'm in a better place, better than you can ever imagine. Take care of yourself, until we meet again. Tell my sister that I love her."

About an hour later, my cousin came over. I was happy just to hear her voice in the house. Out of my anger and grief, I instructed her to bag all of Andre's clothes. The pain was too great for me to even look at his clothes. And, I thought, what good are the clothes without the owner?

I went into my room. I just wanted to be left alone to my thoughts, and try to get some sleep. My body was signaling me that I needed rest, but my mind was not in agreement. There were so many things going through my head that would not allow sleep to come.

I had not addressed the issues of what had really happened. Who did it and why did my baby have to die like that? Then came the what if. If I had put him on punishment, maybe this would not have happened. Why didn't I see all the warning signs? Then I thought about the strange feeling that came over me when I stepped out of the car. I now believe that was a release of our earthly ties with Andre. It was just too overwhelming for me to even think about. Sometime in the middle of the night, I drifted off to sleep.

Now it was dawn. I continued to lie in bed, full of grief, and feeling sorry for myself. I did not know how I was going to face this day without my child. I was hoping that when the morning came, I would wake up from a bad dream and Andre would be at my door, saying, "Mom, could I do this or can I do that?" But the reality is that he was gone.

My daughter came into my bedroom. I knew she wanted to talk. Suddenly I began to feel bad because I had only thought of my own pain. Here I was, isolated in my room, feeling sorry for myself, not realizing that she had suffered the same loss. She was in pain too. And worried about me. That was a little bit too much for a young child to have to endure. I again assured her that I was okay. But we both expressed how much we missed Andre, and we cried together. I listened as she expressed her hurt. She wanted to know why God took her only brother and left her alone. Why couldn't God have taken a brother from another family where there were many children? She said, "That was my friend. Now I have no one." I told

her that I did not have the answer. But I reminded her that I lost my only son. But, thank
God, I still had a daughter and she still had a
mother. So, we had each other.

Chapter 8

I dreaded the days that lay ahead. Just the thought of making funeral arrangements made my stomach churn. But having my family and friends by my side made those days bearable.

I recalled a statement, that I had heard so many times, that now carried so much truth and so much weight. It states, "Give me my flowers while I am alive, so that I can enjoy them." It was not until I was in the middle of a nightmare that I truly understood those words.

In times like these, if we are not careful, we can let our emotions control our decision-making. And in many cases, we may find ourselves spending too much money, unnecessarily, on funeral arrangements. Of course, we all want our loved ones put away nicely. And we can do this, without it costing an arm and a leg.

Many times, guilt comes into play for one reason or another. Perhaps because of something we did or failed to do while the person was alive. We may now feel that the funeral provides an opportunity for restitution. And, we end up spending an enormous amount on the funeral arrangements.

Well, hold on to your checkbook, because you are a bit too late. That person is gone and the dead will never benefit from any amount of money that you spend on the arrangements. Nor will they enjoy the flowers. That's why they say give them their flowers while they are alive so that they can enjoy them. Don't wait until a person is dead to try to do something nice for them.

I did not expect to hear some of the prices that I was quoted. Some of the prices in my opinion were quite expensive. Like trying to buy a Rolls Royce when you only needed a Volkswagen. At one point I was tempted to go with the Rolls Royce even though there were cheaper prices. Thank God I came to my senses and went with what I could afford.

The best advice I can give is to treat others the way you would like to be treated, so that you will not be faced with that problem. Don't put off until tomorrow what you can do today, because tomorrow is not promised to any of us. Today is a gift, that's why it is called the present. Make every day you have count. If there is something that you want to give to someone or do for someone or say to someone, do it now if it is at all in your power. Don't take your life, your family's lives, or your friend's lives for granted. Don't be faced with these words: I started to do that or something told me to do that, but I did not listen. Someone is trying to tell you something. You will never know when that good-bye will be the last good-bye. Don't put yourself in a strain by trying to impress other people. Do what is comfortable for you within your budget. Believe me, the service will be nice. And besides, I have never heard comments on how cheap a casket was.

I don't believe people go to a funeral concerned about how much money was spent on it. They may go to see who is in attendance. Most people attend funeral services out of love and respect for the dead and the family. And hopefully, people use it as a reminder that we all have to die. People are probably thanking God that it was not their turn. But we need to realize that our turn will come, and we need to be ready when that time comes. No man knows the hour or the minute when death will occur. The Bible says, "Behold, I come like a thief in the night." So, live your life as if today is the last day because one day it will be.

Chapter 9

Two days after Andre's death, I received a call from the detectives handling the case. We made an appointment for them to stop by that evening. I was hoping that they would be able to shed some light on the situation, because I knew very little about my child's death.

The detectives arrived about 5. They introduced themselves and handed me their card. They appeared very pleasant and concerned. After taking a seat, they began by showing us a composite drawing of the suspect.

They said the picture was drawn based on information that was given to them by the witnesses. But they warned us that it might not be an accurate description. They told me that the picture had been posted throughout the neighborhood in hopes that someone would recognize the suspect and come forth.

I CRY NO MORE

Neither my daughter nor I recognized the face. They questioned my daughter and me. But, I did not have much to contribute other than what they already knew.

So basically, I listened while the detectives and my daughter spoke. My daughter said that she was at home when she received the news from a friend, who rode his bike to our house to let her know that Andre had been shot. She rode to the scene of the crime on his handlebars. When they got there, Andre was lying on the ground unconscious.

One of Andre's friends, who witnessed the shooting, told her that they were standing in the alley that ran alongside his friend's house. They were laughing and talking when an old beat up car drove into the alley. There was a man and woman inside the car. They pointed their gun, and asked if anyone wanted to die? When my daughter was telling this, I thought, "What a question to ask." Apparently, the man pulled the trigger, but the gun didn't go off. When the gun clicked, Andre's friend said, "Come on, Andre, let's go." But, for some reason, Andre just stood there. The next time the man pulled the trigger, the gun went off and shot him.

The detectives believed it was a gang initiation. I don't believe we were any help, and frankly, neither were they. As they prepared to leave, they said they would keep us informed and, if we heard anything, we should feel free to call them.

About a week later, we were informed by one of Andre's friends that a letter was sent to the boy who lived on Mullen, stating that they were sorry they had shot the wrong person. It was him they were after. Not long after Andre's death, that family moved.

It had been one week since we buried Andre. My daughter and I were doing the best we could to try and comfort each other. Sometimes that can be very difficult, especially when you are in pain yourself.

On that day, I found myself lying in the bed feeling sorry for myself. As I was lying there, I heard a voice say, "You had better get out of that bed, because you have a daughter to take care of and bills to pay. Who do you think is going to take care of those things for you?" It was at that moment, that reality kicked in. Those things had not crossed my mind. I hopped up, and immediately started tending to my business. I guess that was all I needed – just to hear a word from God. I can truly say, it was a step in the right direction for me. Because this time, I listened.

Chapter 10

For such a long time, I kept asking myself, why is it that I couldn't see any of the warning signs? They were as plain as day. What is it that made me so blind? I began rationalizing, maybe this or maybe that, but nothing I came up with seemed to make sense. One morning, I flicked on the television, and there was a minister talking about fear. He said that fear was based on something that had happened in our past. At that point, he really got my attention. Huh! I thought to myself, that's quite interesting. His message made me think again. My past seemed to have been okay to me. The only thing that I could think of that had a real effect on my life was the death of my father.

Lord! No sooner did that thought entered my mind, than all the lights came on. My mind opened up to a brighter day. That's it! Then I remembered, that feeling that I experienced the day that my father died, was the same feeling I experienced 37 years later when my son died. I knew the same spirit, the spirit of death, had contacted me. Things were coming together and beginning to have real meaning for me. Oh, my God, I had no idea. After all those years, the simple message that I had just heard on television carried so much power. It was the key that unlocked the door to my mind. But, why had it taken so long? Now that I know what I know, whatever else I needed to know would follow. It's all in line with the word of God which says, "Ask, and it shall be given, seek, and ye shall find; knock, and it shall be opened unto you." Yes, I wanted to know and at that moment, I knew.

Chapter 11

My father died a young man in his thirties. I was young myself, but I still remember that day as if it happened only yesterday. The morning of his death, my father woke me before he went to work and asked me if I'd do a favor for him. Of course, I said, "Yes." I loved my daddy very much. He asked me to iron his shirt. I did, and didn't give it any thought. It wasn't like him to be unprepared; he must have been running late for work. I ironed his shirt, he thanked me, and then he gave me some money. I was as happy as I could be.

Before leaving for work that day, my father received a call regarding a change in plans. He and his friends had planned to go fishing the next day, on Tuesday. But at the last minute, they changed it to that day, Monday. This change came as a real surprise to him. He kept asking my mother, "I wonder why they changed it?" It seemed to have been a big concern for him. Shortly thereafter, my parents left for work.

My father always drove my mother to and from work because she did not know how to drive. Usually when my parents returned from work in the evening, they followed a routine. But that evening was different from any evening I could remember. My father rushed into the house, checked on us to make sure everything was okay, then changed his clothes for his fishing trip.

He didn't even take the time to eat dinner. The only time I can ever remember him not eating was when he was sick and that was not often. To me, he acted as if time was of the essence and that he had a deadline that he could not be late for.

When my father started to leave that night, my young brother, who was 5 years old at the time, started yelling and screaming, begging my father not to go. My father assured him that he would be back. The way my brother carried on that evening, you would have thought someone was killing him. I had never seen him act like that in all the five years he'd been on earth.

The whole thing seemed bizarre to me. How were they going to fish at night? Would they be able to see the fish? But I was young, what did I know?

That night my mother hosted a Stanley Party at our house. She served refreshments while the consultants showed the women the different household products. The women played games and enjoyed themselves in a way that was just good clean fun. I always called it a chat and chew party. I had gone to a Sock Hop at the YMCA with my cousin. We returned home just as the party was ending. Everyone was gone except my aunt and her children. We decided to listen to some music. I was at the record player, sorting through the records, when out of the blue a saddening feeling came over me. This feeling filled my entire body. I said to myself, "Something is getting ready to happen." The feeling lasted only a few seconds. It went as quickly as it came. So, I didn't bother to mention it to anyone. At the time, I did not know why I said what I said, nor why I felt the way I felt. I had never felt that way before. I just remember it as being a saddening and uncomfortable feeling.

About a half-hour later, the phone rang. My aunt answered it and I watched as this strange look came over her face. I knew something was wrong, but I had no idea it was going to be so tragic.

Then, my aunt turned to my mother and said, "Jones. Jones is dead. He drowned." I could not believe my ears! At that moment it did not compute. She was talking about my father! Hey, there was something wrong with this picture. At that point, my mother just slid to the floor in despair. We didn't ask who the caller was. Of course, my aunt knew. But the messenger wasn't important; it was the message that had shattered our lives that night.

I can still remember hearing my baby brother saying, over and over again, "I told him not to go. If he had listened to me, he would not be dead." In just a twinkling of an eye, our happy lives had turned into sadness.

Based on my experience, I believe that my father knew that death was near for him. He may not have known the hour or the minute because Scripture tells us that no man knows the hour or the minute.

About a month before his death, my father had what I called a family lecture, which meant he talked and we listened. He talked about what we needed to do, what he wanted us to do and what he wanted my mother to start doing. He wanted her to start paying the bills and learning how to do other things that he normally took care of. He ended his talk by saying that he wasn't always going to be around.

Sometimes, we would giggle because we thought he was kidding. My brothers and I were young and didn't take his talks seriously. I felt that we would be having family talks over and over again. After all, he was a young man. He was only thirty-seven. I couldn't ever remember a time when my father had been sick, other than an occasional cold or a cut on the hand. To me, he looked like the picture of health.

The only deaths I had experienced were those of older people. So, I just knew that my father would be around to see us grow up and to see his grandchildren. That's the way I thought the story always went. Now, I realize that was just a child's thinking.

A few day after my father's death I recall my mother telling us about the experience she had with my father on the day of his death as he was driving her to work. It was not an ordinary conversation. My father was shouting and continuously repeating the statement that he wanted me to go to college and that he knew my older brother would not go. My mother said he continued his verbal rampage until he dropped her off at work. She could not understand what in the world could have triggered that.

It was all of these things that made me feel that my father knew that his time was running out. He tried strongly to get his point across. He did everything he could to prepare us for that day and thereafter. I didn't understand at the time what was driving him, but now I do. I believe that when that feeling came over me that evening, that was the exact moment my father took his last breath.

Chapter 12

Based on my own experience, I believe that we can manipulate our minds to think and believe anything. We can believe that something is that isn't, that something was when it wasn't. But, at the same time, we keep running further and further from the truth.

In my case, I blocked out everything out of fear. I did not want to hear it, so I created a situation that was bearable for me. It was easy for me to ignore the situation because there was no real evidence that something was going to happen. That was because it came to me as a feeling. But I still lost in the end.

I feel that in most instances it's best to deal with what is at hand and many times we can save ourselves a lot of heartaches and pain. Problems will come, but it's the way we handle them when they come that will have an effect on the future.

It has been thirty-five years since my father's death. Just recently, I began to wonder if anyone else in my family had experienced what I felt the night of his death. I began to ask myself, "Why was I the only one?" It was then that I suddenly realized I had never shared my experience with anyone. How would anyone else know what I experienced, or if I even had an experience, if I did not share it? Sharing the message was not as important to me then as the pain I felt at the loss of my father. Knowing how others felt would not have made a difference. But now there was a need for me to know. I felt that knowing would make a big difference in my life. I am a firm believer that things happen in their own time and space, and when they are most needed. Knowing all of this would not have meant anything to me back then. It was now that I needed to know.

I really didn't want to bring up the past after all these years. But sometimes, there are things that occurred in our past that may be a direct link to what is going on in our future, and it is the truth that shall set us free. I believed that, especially after the experience of my son's death. I was grateful that I had someone I could ask. I called my mother that night.

I was shocked as I listened to the thing she had to say. All I could do was keep quiet.

She told me that on the night of my father's death, right after the party ended, she began to feel really down. Her heart felt heavy, then a strange feeling came over her. She heard a voice saying, "You had better get something to eat now, because later on you won't be able to eat." She said she did not understand what that meant. So, she just cast the thought from her mind. The first thing I said was, "Oh, my God, it happened to you too. I had no idea." When I related my experience to her, she was just as surprised.

She informed me that she shared her experiences with others many times. And, she reminded me that whenever the subject of my father's death came up; I would either leave the room or ask that the subject be changed. I remember that oh so well.

I just wasn't able to handle going over my father's death again and again. It was too painful just knowing that I would have to go through life without a father. I surely wasn't in the mood to entertain people or to see them being entertained. That was the way I felt then, and I did very little talking about my father after that. I have kept my feelings inside of me all these years.

I could not believe my ears. The same thing that happened to me happened to my mother. She had just cast it from her mind like I had done. I guess we all do that. Just brush things aside when we don't understand. But somewhere down the line, we get an understanding of what it was all about. Sometimes it's too late to do anything about it, if in fact, there is anything we can do, other than recognize the fact that we are just being made aware.

When we see clouds in the sky or hear the weather forecast regarding rain, it's not for us to then try and figure out how we can stop the rain from coming. We are just being made aware so that we can be prepared. Some things we just can't change, no matter what we think. It's not always in our power. So therefore, we ask God to grant us the serenity to accept the things we cannot change, the courage to change the things we can, and the wisdom to know the difference.

Chapter 13

My mother asked me if I remembered the visit to our grandparents after we returned from Colorado. I did remember. She went on to say that after we turned off the highway onto the road leading to the house, a voice spoke to her saying, "This will be the last time you will ever come here as a family."

My mother had no idea what that meant. She tried to find answers to ease her mind. She thought it meant something was going to happen to our grandparents. But that did not sound right to her. The message said, as a family, which meant all of us, my mother, father, two brothers and myself. Nothing she came up with seemed to satisfy her. Finally, she cast it from her mind, just as she had done all the other signs.

As I continued to listen, thoughts ran through my mind. I began to reflect on all the signs I had leading up to Andre's death. And now my mother was telling me about her experiences. There had to be more to this than what meets the eye. I didn't know what, but if it was for me to know, I knew I would. I thought I had heard all there was to hear, until she began telling me about the dreams. She said that one morning; my father woke up and began telling her about the horrible dream he had the night before. He said it was about her death. He went on and on about how horrible it was. She said that the way he spoke about it was as if it had already happened. She had to remind him that she was not dead, no matter how real it felt. She could not believe her ears because she had a similar dream that same night, but it was about my father's death. After hearing his dream and the way it affected him, she never mentioned her dream to him. Several nights later, she said my father had a nightmare and shouted out, "Why did yall let me drown?" He never woke up from his sleep. Now that I know all that I know, I can understand the drama my father was going through. We call it dreams, some call it premonitions or intuition, but whatever the case, my father's dream became a reality. He previewed his death through his dream.

My mother even mentioned that my grand-mother, my father's mother, had a dream. She dreamed that a group of boys were swimming in a lake and all of the boys made it back except for one. That one drowned. My grandmother had previewed the death of her son.

I shared with my mother the experience I had one night while I was asleep. My father appeared at the foot of my bed. He was dressed in the same suit he had on when he was buried. He wanted to know how I was doing, and if we had visited his mother? I say it was a dream, but it was so real to me. What made it seem so real to me was that he was dressed in the same suit we buried him in. When I opened my eyes, he was gone. The Bible says there is no com-munication between the dead and the living. So, I will leave it at that.

After we finished talking about dreams, I thought to myself that it seemed that the messages that we receive in the middle of the night when we are asleep are just as important as the messages we receive during the day when we are wide awake.

My mother and I talked for at least an hour. I knew in her heart that she was probably wondering, why is this girl asking all of these questions after all these years? After all these years, talking about my son's and father's deaths still bring tears to my eyes. I know it was still hard for my mother. But she hung in there. The conversation was beginning to wind down, when she remembered the discussion she and my father had about her purchasing new rugs for the house. He thought that it was a great idea to buy new rugs. But, she wanted his imput. He told her to get the rugs she wanted because he would not need a rug. My mother thought, "What a thing to say. What is he talking about?" She was not following his logic, but she left it at that.

We were at the point of saying our good bye when she said, "Oh, just one more thing and then I will let you go." I was all ears and in no hurry to hang up the phone. That night had been a real awakening for me. My mother said that about a week after we buried my father, a man came to the house. The man said that my father had hired him to paint our house. My mother said she had no knowledge of that. The man went on to say that my father paid him in advance. He added that my father said that he would not be around to complete the job. The man just thought that my father was going on a trip. He said he never imagined anything like my father's death. After my mother told me that, we said good bye and I love you, just as we always did before hanging up.

All I could do was sit there, taking deep breaths and trying to digest everything that I had heard. That conversation with my mother shed much light on many things.

It dawned on me that neither of us mentioned the fact that witnesses said they heard my father yell out for an inner tube, and even though he was close enough to reach for it, he never got it. I believe the same moment my father took his last breath, was the same moment the sad feeling came over me.

He did everything in his power to prepare us for that day and the days to come through his family lectures, words of encouragement, and his attempt to leave no loose ends.

All I can say is that I thank God for allowing Jones Burks to be our father. I don't know much about dreams, premonitions, or what some say is intuition, but what I do know, is that the events that occurred in my life and the lives of my family actually happened.

It just lets me know that God does not let things slip up on us. He always gives us a peek. God still speaks to me everyday and I am becoming a better listener. But not only does he speak to me, he speaks to each and every one of us. Remember the day you made the statement, "I started to do this or that or something told me not to do this or that," and you didn't listen? Then, later on, you realized you made the wrong choice. We have all been there, done that. God wants to direct our path, if we allow Him. He loves us equally and His Words are constant reminders of His Love. He is always with us. Whether we choose to accept it or not, is not an indication of a change in His plan. I believe it's just one way God has of keeping His promises.

Chapter 14

It has been 14 years since my son's death, and his murder has never been solved. And probably never will be. Either way, it will never bring him back. I believe the person who killed my son feels that he has gotten away with murder. But he never got away with it. He just never got caught. I know it has been hell right here on earth for him because he had to live with himself. But I no longer hate him. I have forgiven him and by doing so I am able to go on.

Recently while driving down the street, I saw a billboard that caught my eye. It was announcing the release of a new movie "Eyes Wide Shut." I smiled. That was a good title. I knew, because I had lived that way. I thought I was walking around with my eyes opened, but in reality, I couldn't see anything.

However, I no longer beat myself up or drive myself crazy about that time in my life. There were so many lessons for me in all of this. The biggest one was that death is inevitable. But we learn to grow through our pain and find a way to live on.

That's what I had to do. Find a way to live through two deaths that effected me beyond belief. As I look back on both of these incidents, it's a wonder that I survived. But the thing is, I did survive. Of course I made mistakes, like we all do. I searched for my father in every relationship, but that never works, and with my son I made mistakes there too, but now, I prefer to focus on all the things I did well. And, I have accomplished a lot. So with all of that, the good and the bad, I've made it through this thing we call life. And I am grateful to God for all of the experiences He has sent my way. All that I am is a myriad of all that I've been through. And the truth is, I am winning this race, all by God's grace.

I thank God for bringing me out. And I also thank God for the opportunity to be in the lives of two wonderful people – my son, Andre

Chevel Cunningham, and my father, Jones Burks Jr. When I think of them now, a smile comes to my face because I know that they live in my heart and in my soul. That's why I cry no more.

Sister's Reflections

The date was June 16, 1985; and it was a very sad day for me, because I lost my only brother. I never had a sister, so when I lost my brother that was it. When my mother told me that the doctors weren't able to save my brother's life, a piece of me died also. I immediately blamed God, because to me, it just wasn't fair. He took my only sibling, leaving me alone.

For a long time I was angry with, and hated, God. In my heart, my soul, my mind and my spirit, I felt God could have taken a brother from another family that had many siblings. Instead God took the only one that I had.

One night while I was crying myself to sleep, my brother appeared to me. He said to me, "Don't cry for me; for I am in a better place now, and I'm at peace. Yes, I will see you again." I always kept those thoughts with me. It's strange to say, but I didn't go around certain people when they had gatherings, because I always felt quite uncomfortable. It was hard for me to watch other brothers and sisters fellow-shipping with each other, knowing that I no longer had a brother to fellowship and share with. I felt as if I did not fit in. If people ask me if I had any sisters or brothers, some-times I would say no; other times I would tell people yes. Whenever I replied yes, I felt that I would have to explain my brother's death.

I remember ever so clearly, to this day, when my brother's friend rode his bike up to my Mom's house, crashing his bike into the wall, and shouting, "Anthea!" "Your brother has been shot!" I rode on the handlebars of his bike to the place where my only brother lay on the ground fighting for his young life. I went to him; his eyes were rolling in the back of his head. I hugged and kissed him, I felt so help-less. I was the one that got him out of trouble on many occasions; yet now I was helpless, without the power or the ability to help him. I felt so helpless, because I couldn't do anything for him.

As years went by, I had flashbacks to "that place" where he lay dying on the ground. When-ever I had these flashbacks, which usually left me feelling overwhelmed with sadness, I'd change it with something funny he had done. I began to let God in my life, and that's when my peace, in regards to my brother's death, began. I had to realize that in spite of all, God is good. I also came to know that He, and He alone, could and would give me "the peace that passeth all understanding"; when you seek Him.

BOOK AVAILABLE THROUGH
Milligan Books
An Imprint Of Professional Business
Consulting Service

I Cry No More $12.00

Order Form

Milligan Books
1425 West Manchester, Suite B,
Los Angeles, California 90047
(323) 750-3592

Mail Check or Money Order to:
Milligan Books

Name _____ Date _____

Address _____

City_____ State _____ Zip Code_____

Day telephone _____

Evening telephone_____

Book title _____

Number of books ordered ___ Total cost .... $_____

Sales Taxes (CA Add 8.25%) .... $_____

Shipping & Handling $3.00 per book .... $_____

Total Amount Due..$_____

• Check   • Money Order   Other Cards _____

• Visa   • Master Card   Expiration Date _____

Credit Card No. _____

Driver's License No. _____

Signature   Date

Order Form

Milligan Books
1425 West Manchester, Suite B,
Los Angeles, California 90047
(323) 750-3592

Mail Check or Money Order to:
Milligan Books

Name _____ Date _____

Address _____

City_____ State _____ Zip Code_____

Day telephone _____

Evening telephone_____

Book title _____

Number of books ordered ___ Total cost .... $_____

Sales Taxes (CA Add 8.25%) .... $_____

Shipping & Handling $3.00 per book .... $_____

Total Amount Due..$_____

• Check   • Money Order   Other Cards _____

• Visa   • Master Card   Expiration Date _____

Credit Card No. _____

Driver's License No. _____

Signature   Date